# FOGGY FOREST FRIENDS

BY

KERAH CONSTANTINE-LETREN

In a foggy forest there lived ten trees, one named Maple and one named Greene.

In the fog, the trees slept right

But in the night the trees swapped places

As sun recharged them, they had grinned faces.

In sunset sky they viewed sunflowers

But on rainy days they spread out to protect the flowers.

With thunder and lightning they vibrated.

They portrayed frightful faces.

When in nightfall they corresponded with the constellation,

Switching positions while the sun was on vacation.

The moon illuminated the trees

In the wind they got startled with breeze

A dust of rain made them startle again.

As the twinkling stars shone brightly,

The fog and the mist appeared nightly.

In that foggy forest there was another tree.

His name was Oak and he was green.

Greene saw oak and said "Hey Oak!"

Oak saw Greene and said "Hey Greeeene!"

staring at his leaves strangely

Greene looked deranged, he was an evergreen turning
brown.

Greene needed help which made Oak yelp.

Maple came along and asked, "what's wrong?"

He gazed and replied, "It's fall, you clowns!"

"FALL?" they questioned.

Maple responded, "Fall is on its way"

Oak wondered "Who's Fall again?"

"It starts in two days" Maple announced.

It was then they understood the season was changing.

The shadiest tree in the fog is Willow.

Once she made Olive wither for spite by dimming her sunlight.

Some trees think Willow is blight because her leaves are covered in white.

Despite the sight, Willow denies it and says it is her birthright.

The two of them stay in constant motion.

They both live alongside the ocean, on the farther side of the forest.

Willow is not an Asian tree

Though others think she has Asian genes.

Her slender branches drape, almost touching her stalk.

Meanwhile, Olive dislikes her mohawk and spikes

Yet still, Olives are a delight.

As they continued to fight, the other trees became involved to correct the wrong.

First Cotton marched down with her woolly hair looking like a cloud.

Second darted Pod but some of his green peas fell onto the grassy ground

Then Pine followed along with his pointy cones woody and brown.

In the veiled fog they spotted Willow and Olive.

They were playing tug of war with each other's branches.

Cotton, Pod and Pine noticed the gloom of the sky.

Suddenly, it turned dark and grey

Even though they liked the perfume of the rain,

They hiked back north to avoid the falling hail.

On their way up they played a game.

It was unlike tug of war

Instead, it was log the slug;

The slowest tree had to roll like a log for moving like a slug.

That tree would gain bugs in their shrubs

And dirt in their skirt.

Thunder roared deafening at the forest.

It shook the dislike out of Willow and Olive

It led them to hug in one grumbling sound.

Afraid if they frowned, a herbivorous iguana would crawl out.

After fall, winter brought its freezing weather.

Willow and Olive began working together.

They cooperated to keep their branches alive

Using all their efforts to escape frostbite,

Refusing to die during the cold winter

Peace between rivals to ease their wither.

They made plans to view the last two poui trees bloom for springtime together.

Soon the fog would clear out

The colourful nature would show.

Strawberries and flowers would grow,

to capture the eyes of insects and hummingbirds.

The flowers of the poui trees, pink and yellow were most impressive.

They wore beautiful and vibrant headdresses, thick and majestic.

Springtime came and the other trees noticed willow and Olive stopped bickering.

Now they were dancing in the wind,

this was the happiest they've been.

For a long time, they remained in their glee.

They became best friends, a flourishing forest's dream.

Forgetting their woes and releasing their bitterness.

All the trees in the forest agreed

You might be a smile away from meeting the tree you need.

It was nice to see the fuzzy forest fog beam.

After Willow and Olive's plight, all the fog had lifted to congratulate their unite.

The sky above was blue again and the once foggy forest stopped seeing rainy days.

THE END

# BOOK INSPIRATION

## Kerah Constantine-Letren

### Foggy Forest Friends

This fantastic story was inspired by my journey to school while riding the bus. Around 6:45 AM one early morning before sunrise, I glimpsed out the small, compact window of the bus I rode. What I saw was a story unfolding in front of me. I felt a sudden urge to tell it. I took my phone out and made a note titled "Foggy Forest Trees", holding that vivid foggy forest in mind as it told its own story. It was simple to envision the fog which clothed these forest trees. If the bus had stopped, I'd have wandered into the forest myself and speak to those trees. They were mainly pinecone trees, found in South Georgia.

I grew up in a rural environment on a mountain which had plentiful fruit trees and other plants surrounding my home. Often, my cousins and I would trail the gardens, raid the star fruit (five finger) and cherry trees and even cruise the other side of the mountain for an adventure. It didn't come as a surprise to me when this story was nature-based, it was more like destiny directing me back home. When I thought about this story, I felt intrinsically encouraged to keep working on it and I pushed myself to add to it until I became satisfied. During the months of springtime, Poui trees normally bloom. Pink and yellow are most common in the Queens Park Savannah of Port of Spain, Trinidad. They are extremely vibrant that they can be spotted from afar. Whenever near to them, especially the yellow ones, I take a picture. Now, I can include it and share it with every owner of this book, wherever they live.

# AUTHOR BIO

Kerah Constantine-Letren is a young Trinidadian-born writer whose passion for reflective-expression emerged during her early childhood. Before turning ten, she took two creative writing summer classes, never imagining their influence would endure. Growing up near to nature, her words recreate nature building worlds. While she recalls little of what she learned, the experience shaped her approach to writing and continues to guide her work today. Foggy Forest Friends initiates her writing career.